# OUR MOON

## NEW DISCOVERIES ABOUT EARTH'S CLOSEST COMPANION

## ELAINE SCOTT

CLARION BOOKS
Houghton Mifflin Harcourt
Boston New York

For my daughter, Susan, whom I love to the moon and back

Clarion Books
215 Park Avenue South
New York, New York 10003

Clarion Books is an imprint of Houghton Mifflin Harcourt Publishing Company.
www.hmhco.com

The text was set in Plantin.

Library of Congress Cataloging-in-Publication Data
Scott, Elaine, 1940– author.
Our moon : new discoveries about Earth's closest companion / Elaine Scott.
pages cm.
Summary: "Full of captivating, kid-friendly information, *Our Moon* covers everything from the newest theories on how
the moon formed, to the recent, startling discovery of water on its surface and the very real possibility of
future moon colonies. Illustrated with full-color photographs and packed with fun facts, this is the
most complete and up-to-date book available on the moon. Includes glossary, bibliography,
and index"—Provided by publisher.
Audience: Ages 9-12.
Includes bibliographical references and index.
ISBN 978-0-547-48394-8 (hardcover)
1. Space flight to the moon—Juvenile literature. 2. Moon—Juvenile
literature. 3. Moon—Exploration—Juvenile literature. 4. Earth
(Planet)—Juvenile literature. I. Title.
TL799.M6S26 2015
523.3—dc23
2015006855
Manufactured in China
SCP 10 9 8 7 6 5 4 3 2
4500590738

Title page Image: A "supermoon"
photographed on July 18, 2008.
Supermoons occur when the moon
is full and its orbit carries it closest to
Earth, causing it to appear bigger
and brighter than ever in the
night sky. The scientific term for
this close approach is perigee.
The moon's orbit around Earth
varies from an average
distance of 225,623 miles
at perigee to an average
of 252,088 miles from
Earth at its farthest point,
or apogee. (NASA/Sean
Smith)

# CONTENTS

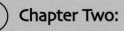

# INTRODUCTION

ON JULY 20, 1969, astronaut Michael "Mike" Collins sat at the controls of *Columbia,* the space vehicle that had carried him and his two fellow astronauts Neil Armstrong (1930–2012) and Edwin "Buzz" Aldrin (1930–) to the moon. Neil and Buzz had left *Columbia* and were already on the moon, making their first explorations of its strange and powdery surface. After much serious communication between Mission Control in Houston, Texas, and the history-making astronauts of Apollo 11, a voice from Houston again crackled into Mike's headset.

*Mission Control: Among the large headlines concerning Apollo this morning, there's one asking that you watch for a lovely girl with a big rabbit. An ancient legend says a beautiful Chinese girl called Chang-o has been living there for 4,000 years. It seems she was banished to the moon because she stole the pill of immortality from her husband. You might also look for her companion, a large Chinese rabbit, who is easy to spot, since he is always standing on his hind feet in*

A full moon lightens the
darkness of the night.
(Jon Sullivan)

Chang-o, now more commonly known as Chang'e, the Chinese moon goddess. (Library of Congress)

Stonehenge, the mysterious ring of stones in Wiltshire, England, may have been used as a type of observatory by people living more than 4,500 years ago. (Bernard Gagnon)

*the shade of a cinnamon tree. The name of the rabbit is not recorded.*

*Collins: Okay. We'll keep a close eye out for the bunny girl.*

Of course, that communication was a joke. The mission was going well, and there was time for a little fun. No one thought there was a Chinese princess or a big rabbit on the moon. Not in 1969. But four thousand years before, in ancient China, when people looked at the full moon and saw the dark markings on its surface, they created many stories to explain them, including the one about Chang-o.

Other ancient cultures created stories about those dark spots on the moon too. One tale sees the man in the moon as a biblical figure. The story in the Bible says Cain killed his brother Abel while they lived in Eden with their parents, Adam and Eve. As punishment for the crime, Cain was banished from his home to a land "east of Eden." A legend developed that the land "east of Eden" was the moon and that Cain was sent there to live, doomed to orbit Earth forever, gazing at the planet he could no longer inhabit because of his terrible crime.

These stories, passed from generation to generation over thousands of years, tell us that the moon has fascinated humans from the beginning of our history. Not only did our ancestors tell stories and sing songs about the glowing disk that moved across the sky each night; some of their civilizations even worshiped the moon, building temples and pyramids in its honor. Others took a scientific interest and created monuments in an attempt to study and measure the moon's phases—the cycle in which it appears to change shape in the night sky. Many scientists believe that Stonehenge, the curious ring of stones on Salisbury Plain in England that was built around 2500 B.C., was a kind of observatory that helped ancient people mark the phases of the sun and the midsummer and midwinter solstices. Thousands of years later, around A.D. 1000, the Anasazi people of the American Southwest carved astronomical markings that measured the movements of the sun and moon into Fajada Butte in Chaco Canyon, New Mexico. These sites—and many more—are open to the public, and it's fun to visit them, think about the past, and

Fajada Butte in Chaco Canyon, New Mexico, was a sacred astronomical site for the Anasazi. (National Park Service)

# Quick Moon Facts

**diameter:** approximately 2,160 miles/3,476 km

**circumference at equator:** 6,783.5 miles/10,917 km
The moon is the fifth largest planetary satellite in our solar system.

**temperature range:** approximately –250°F to 250°F

**orbit speed:** The moon orbits Earth at an average of 2,287 miles per hour/3,680.5 km per hour.

**orbit circumference:** The moon's trip around Earth is approximately 1,499,618 miles/2,413,402 km long.

**orbit length:** 27.3 days

**average distance from Earth:** 238,855 miles/384,400 km

**point at which moon is closest to Earth (perigee):** 225,623 miles/363,104 km

**point at which moon is farthest from Earth (apogee):** 252,088 miles/405,696 km

- If it were possible to travel to the moon by car, it would take 135 days. Traveling at the speed of light would take 1.23 seconds.
- The moon is moving away from Earth at a rate of about 1.5 inches/3.8 cm per year.

SOURCE: (NASA)

# Phases of the Moon

**3. first quarter:** Sometimes called a half moon, only the moon's right side is visible during this phase.

**4. waxing gibbous:** The moon is larger than a first quarter moon, but not full.

**2. waxing crescent:** The right side of the moon becomes visible as a crescent shape in the sky.

**5. full:** The near side of the moon is completely visible.

**1. new:** The moon is not visible from Earth. This is also sometimes called a dark moon.

**6. waning gibbous:** The moon begins to wane, or appear smaller.

**8. waning crescent:** The left side of the crescent is visible.

**7. last quarter:** The left side of the moon is visible.

(NASA)

The eight phases of the moon are named for the "shapes" the moon takes in the night sky. Of course, the moon never really changes shape. It just looks like it does, depending on how much of the near side of the moon is illuminated by the sun at different times in the moon's orbit.

These descriptions tell how the phases appear to people looking at the moon from the Northern Hemisphere. From the Southern Hemisphere, it's just the opposite: during the waxing phase, the left side is illuminated, and during the waning phase, the right side is illuminated.

marvel at our ancestors' efforts to learn more about the mysteries of the moon.

Many of the ancient tales, like the stories of Chang-o and Cain and Abel, share dark and frightening themes, in which the moon is often portrayed as a distant, forbidding place, a kind of outer-space prison or punishment for misbehaving humans. The ancient temples dedicated to the moon can be equally scary; some contain altars upon which archaeologists believe human sacrifice took place. But the truth is, Earth's closest companion in the solar system is actually a good neighbor, not frightening at all. Its light provides guidance on otherwise dark nights, its daily rhythms control the tides of Earth's oceans, and its monthly phases mark off segments of time into months and seasons, helping farmers from ancient days to the present know when to plant and harvest their crops.

Although manned missions to the moon ended in 1972, scientific missions have continued through the years. Today lunar scientists send unmanned missions to the moon in order to learn more about how our solar system—including our planet, Earth—formed 4.5 billion years ago.

It is our nature as human beings to ask questions and seek answers about the universe we live in. Some of those answers lie on the moon, so scientists will continue to study our lunar companion for generations to come. And humans plan to someday walk on its surface again.

## Blue Moon

The term "blue moon" has nothing to do with color. The lunar cycle is 29.5 days, but since we don't measure half-days in our months, our calendars are not always synchronized with the moon. Therefore, about once every three years, the full moon will appear twice in one calendar month—the second appearance is the blue moon. Interestingly, there will never be a blue moon in February, because that month does not have enough calendar days to allow it to happen. The expression "once in a blue moon" has come to describe any rare event.

# CHAPTER ONE

# MAPPING THE MOON

WHEN OUR ANCIENT ancestors looked up at the full moon, they relied on their own eyes to interpret what they saw and on their imaginations to fill in the blanks. There were no scientific instruments, such as telescopes, to help the earliest astronomers identify the craters, volcanoes, and fields of lava that cover the moon's surface. And so it is amazing that 2,500 years ago, even without a telescope, there were people who were able to make remarkably correct assumptions about Earth's nearest neighbor. One of these ancient thinkers was the philosopher Anaxagoras (circa 500–428 B.C.), who was born in Smyrna in what is now Izmir, Turkey. Anaxagoras traveled to Athens, Greece, where he became a teacher, as well as a great friend of Pericles, who headed the government in Athens at the time. Anaxagoras is remembered because he urged his students not only to rely on their senses (what they could see, touch, taste, or hear) but also to use logic and reason (their minds) as they tried to understand their world.

Giovanni Battista Riccioli's map of the moon, as it appeared in his book *Almagestum novum* (*New Almagest*), published in 1651. (Adler Collection)

Aristotle was a great teacher who said, "All men by nature desire to know." (Jusepe de Ribera, The Clowes Collection, Indianapolis Museum of Art)

Using logic and reasoning, Anaxagoras came up with many new and radical ideas, among them that the moon's light is not produced by the moon. Anaxagoras suggested that moonlight is really a reflection of the sun's light bouncing off the moon. Although he was correct, Anaxagoras's ideas—like many ideas that are new and different—were not warmly welcomed by everyone. In fact, he was arrested and was going to be put to death for his new ways of thinking. But his friend Pericles helped him escape back to Smyrna where he finished out his life in peace. Around one hundred years later, the Greek philosopher Aristotle (384–322 B.C.) claimed he began to form his own understanding and knowledge of science by studying the work of Anaxagoras.

Almost two thousand years after Aristotle, in the 1500s, Europe was in the middle of a period known as the Renaissance. There was a new interest in art and science. The printing press had been invented, and more and more people learned to read. Some were even wearing glasses to see better! In the early 1600s, a Dutch lensmaker, Hans Lippershey (LIP-er-shy) (1570–1619) was working with his lenses and discovered that if he held one lens in front of another and looked through both at the same time, objects appeared larger and closer than they really were. Since it was inconvenient to hold lenses apart, Lippershey put one lens on each end of a tube, making it much easier to look through both lenses at once. Although others may have been doing similar work in other places, Lippershey applied for a patent and is credited with being the inventor of the telescope.

# Thinking Logically

Logic is a method of using reason to reach a conclusion. Ancient Greek philosophers often used a form of reasoning called a syllogism to prove a point. A syllogism is a three-step argument that says if statement A is true, and statement B is true, then it follows that statement C, which is a conclusion, must be true too. However, it is important to remember that the first two statements in a syllogism have to be accurate in order for them to lead to an accurate conclusion. For example:

Statement A: Everyone on my team knows how to play soccer.

Statement B: My best friend is on my team.

Statement C: Therefore, my best friend knows how to play soccer.

However, if some on your team are just beginning to learn how to play the game, then statement A isn't accurate, and that means that the conclusion may not be accurate either. This type of conclusion is called a syllogism fallacy.

Although Anaxagoras, Aristotle, and the other teachers and philosophers of ancient Greece greatly contributed to our understanding of the world, their reasoning wasn't always correct and they created fallacies, or incorrect conclusions, too. For example, Aristotle and most of his contemporaries thought the universe itself was a giant sphere, or ball, and that like any ball it had an edge, or boundary, to it. In other words, it was finite. Aristotle also thought Earth was at the very center of this "ball" and that the sun, moon, planets, and stars were also perfect spheres that occupied their own separate circular "tracks" around Earth, a little like the separate lanes on a racing track. To the ancient Greeks a smooth sphere was the perfect shape. A syllogism that explains Aristotle's thinking about the moon might look like this:

Statement A: All heavenly objects are perfectly round spheres.

Statement B: The moon is a heavenly object.

Statement C: Therefore, the moon is a perfectly round sphere.

For Aristotle and his followers, that syllogism would have made sense, and as a result they believed the moon was a smooth round ball. Of course, almost 2,400 years after Aristotle, we know the first statement of the syllogism is incorrect. Asteroids, for example, are not round, and the conclusion about the moon is incorrect too.

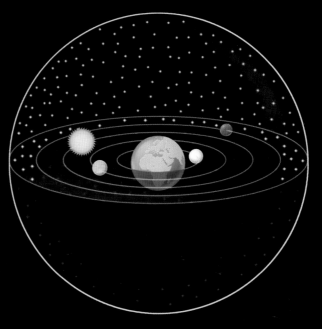

Aristotle believed that the planets of our solar system orbited around Earth, not the sun. Aristotle was wrong.
(Rob Schuster)

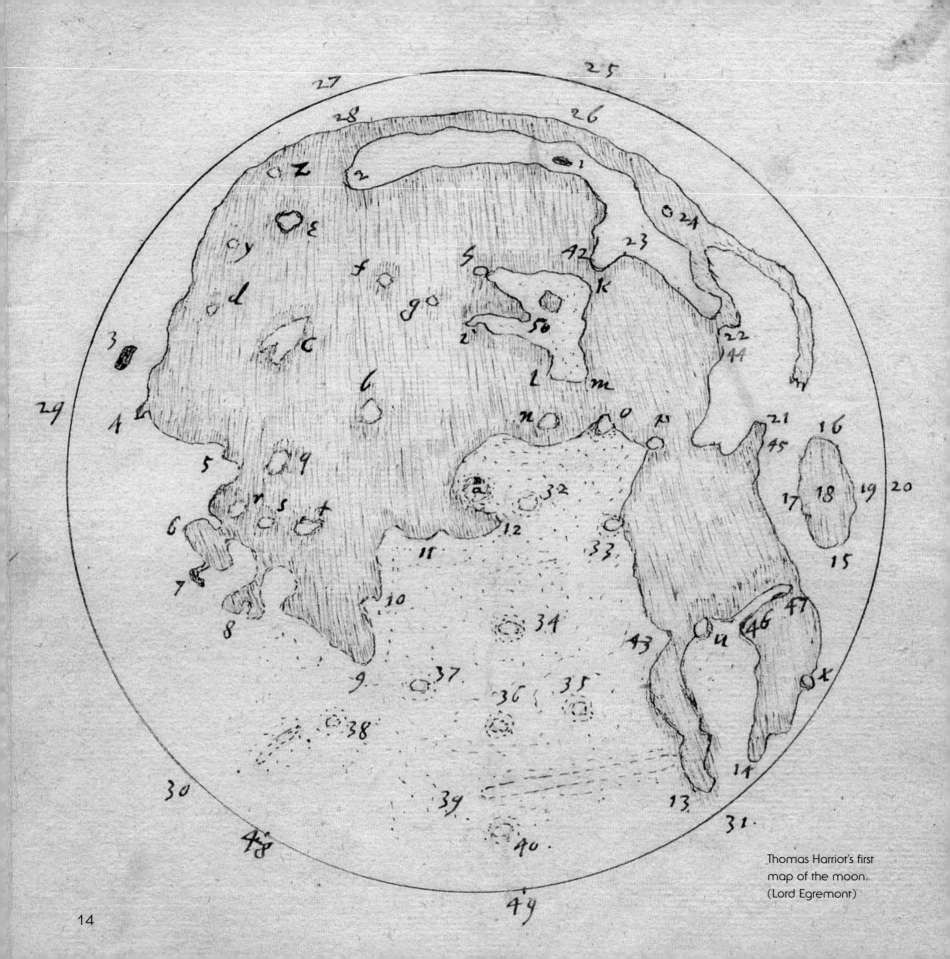

Thomas Harriot's first
map of the moon.
(Lord Egremont)

14

By 1609 news of this invention had spread across Europe and Great Britain. In England an astronomer named Thomas Harriot (1560–1621) became the first scientist to use a telescope to study the moon. As Harriot studied the lunar surface, he drew maps of what he observed. But knowledge that comes from new discoveries has little use if it isn't shared with others. For some reason, Thomas Harriot wasn't eager to publish his work, so his discoveries about the moon's surface and the maps he drew remained largely unknown.

Meanwhile, in Italy, another astronomer was hard at work with his telescope. His name was Galileo Galilei (ga-luh-LAY-oh ga-luh-LAY-ee) (1564–1642). Galileo had built his own telescope, and he used it to study the moon. As he gazed at the moon's surface night after night, Galileo was able to watch the way the sun's light caused shadows as it fell on the moon's mountains, valleys, craters, and plains. Galileo came to a conclusion: the moon was *not* the perfectly smooth sphere that Aristotle and others had claimed it was.

Unlike Harriot, Galileo was eager to publish his discoveries, and after a few short months of observing the moon he wrote about what he had learned. As a result Galileo is given credit for being the first to make these discoveries. To this day, in science as well as in other fields of study, scholars must, in order to be considered expert, find a way to publish their research, allowing others to test and confirm it, so eventually everyone can learn from it.

In the years following the work of Harriot and Galileo, other

One of Galileo's first telescopes. (NASA)

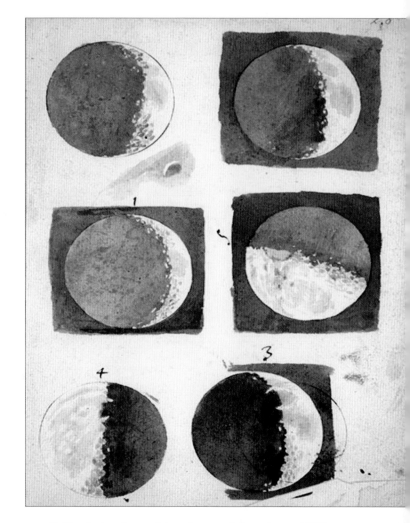

Galileo's drawings of the phases of the moon, 1609. (Ministero dei beni e delle attività culturali e del tuismo/ Biblioteca Nationale Centrale di Firenze)

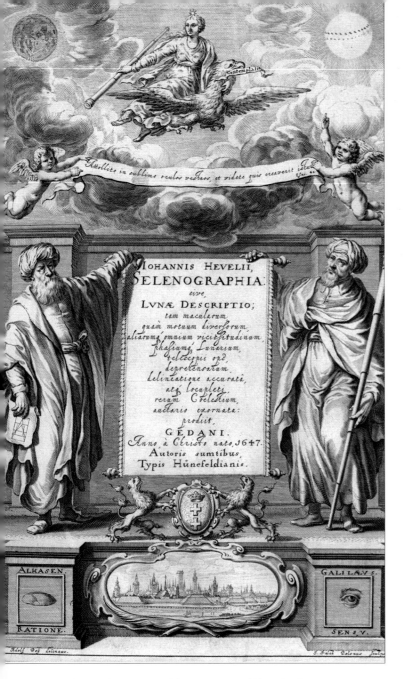

The elaborately engraved frontispiece of Hevelius's *Selenographia*, published in 1647. Ibn al-Haytham, one of the greatest Muslim scholars of his time, stands on the left, holding a geometrical diagram that symbolizes gaining knowledge through reason. Galileo stands on the right, holding a telescope, to symbolize gaining knowledge through use of the senses. (Houghton Library, Harvard University)

astronomers were drawn to the moon and its mysteries. In 1645, the Belgian astronomer and mapmaker Michael Florent van Langren (circa 1600–1675) drew the first known map of the moon that placed all of its individual features in an accurate location. And in 1647 a wealthy Polish brewer, Johannes Hevelius (1611–1687), who had been studying the moon for years and drawing and making engravings of what he saw, gave a name to this process of mapping the moon—*selenography.* Selene is the name for the Greek goddess of the moon, and Hevelius titled his book *Selenographia.* There were no cameras then, but Hevelius's astonishing and detailed engravings showed the astronomers of his day—and those in the decades that followed him—how to accurately use light and shadow to illustrate not just the moon but all the stars, planets, and other celestial bodies they were studying.

In his engravings, Hevelius named some of the features he saw on the moon, but credit for naming most of them belongs to another Italian astronomer, Giovanni Battista Riccioli (1598–1671). Riccioli was a Jesuit priest who worked closely with his much younger student and fellow Jesuit, Francesco Maria Grimaldi (1618–1663). After studying the earlier work of Langren and Hevelius, Riccioli and Grimaldi eventually published their own maps created from their personal observations in a book called *Almagestum novum* (*New Almagest*). Although Riccioli acknowledged Grimaldi's contributions to the book, only Riccioli's name appears as its author.

In the book, the men named the craters of the moon's northern hemisphere after famous astronomers of the past, including Ptolemy and Copernicus. They named the craters in the south after famous men who were living at that time. However, neither Riccioli nor Grimaldi understood exactly what he was looking at when observing the moon. The dark-colored areas on the moon's surface looked like smooth seas to them, so they called each of these a *mare*, which is the Latin word for "sea." And they named one large, dark rounded area *Mare Tranquillitatis*, or the Sea of Tranquility.

As centuries passed, planetary scientists eventually learned that the dark spots on the moon's surface—its *maria*, which is the plural for *mare*—were not seas at all. By the time the astronauts of the Apollo missions were making their trips to the moon, scientists knew these "seas" were lowlands, smooth areas often marked with round craters that have been filled in with basalt—lava from ancient volcanoes. Riccioli's *Mare Tranquillitatis* was one of those craters. It became the most famous location on the moon when, on July 20, 1969, Neil Armstrong and Buzz Aldrin prepared to land the *Eagle* there. That landing, however, was not exactly tranquil.

## GEOCENTRIC OR HELIOCENTRIC?
# Competing Views of the Universe

About 450 years after Aristotle, another Greek astronomer and teacher, Ptolemy (TOLE-uh-me) (A.D. 100–179) taught that Earth was at the center of the universe as they understood it and that the sun and all the planets orbited, or circled, Earth. This view of the solar system is called the geocentric theory, because *geo* is Greek for "earth." The geocentric theory of the solar system was widely accepted until the Polish astronomer Nicolaus Copernicus (Co-PER-ni-cus) (1473–1543) claimed the sun, not Earth, was at the center of our solar system, and that all the planets in our solar system orbit it. Copernicus's new ideas were not widely accepted in his lifetime. Working a hundred years after Copernicus, the Italian astronomer Galileo Galilei was able to use a brand-new instrument—the telescope—to observe the heavens, and he supported Copernicus's idea of a heliocentric solar system. *Helios* is the Greek word for "sun." "Centric" comes from the Greek word *kentron*, which means "of the center."

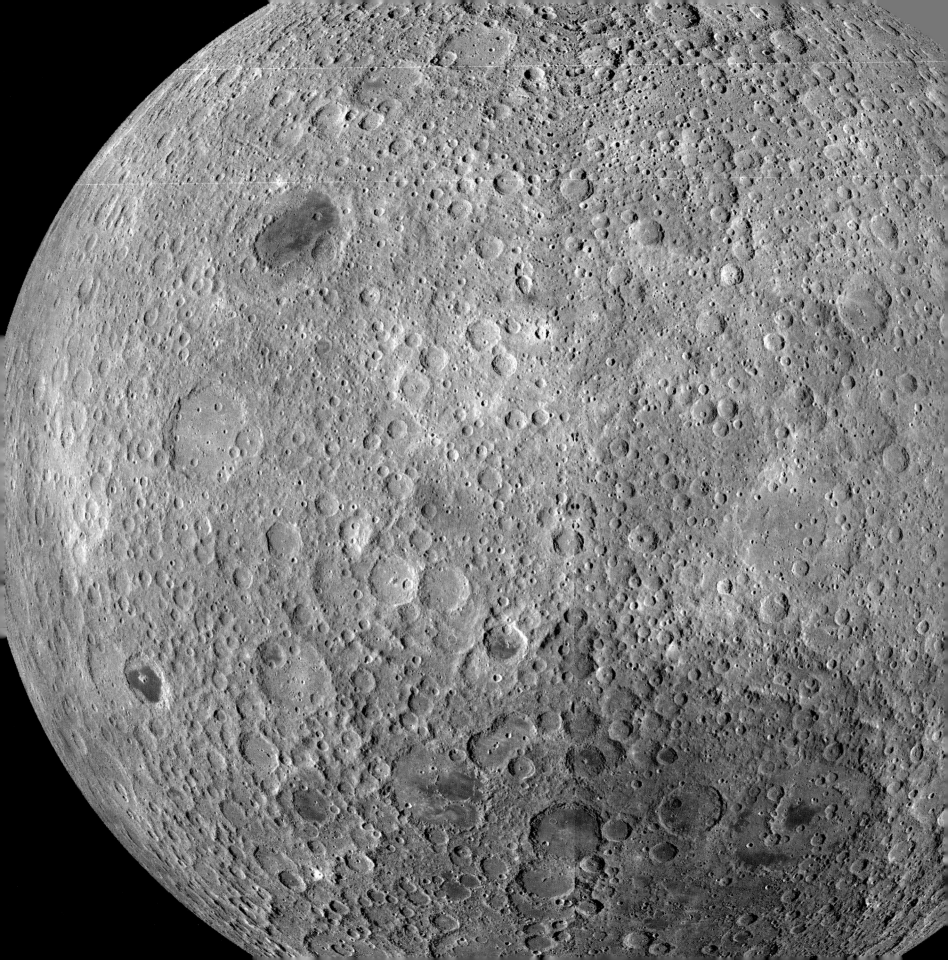

# CHAPTER TWO

# EARTH'S SISTER

The far side of the moon. The first people to see it with their own eyes were the crew of Apollo 11. (NASA/Goddard/Arizona State University)

MIKE COLLINS, Neil Armstrong, and Buzz Aldrin flew over the far side, or "dark side," of the moon on July 20, 1969. No humans had ever before seen it with their own eyes, because the same side of the moon always faces Earth as the moon orbits our planet.

The three astronauts must have been tempted to take a good long look at the dark side of the moon as they rocketed past it, but there was no time for gawking. They were busy. It was time to prepare for the descent to the Sea of Tranquility, and humankind's first steps onto another heavenly body. Neil Armstrong and Buzz Aldrin wedged themselves into the tiny landing craft, the *Eagle*. *Columbia* continued its orbit, passing over the near side of the moon. The carefully chosen landing site, called Tranquility base, came into view. At precisely the right moment, Mike Collins pressed a button that activated a set of springs. The spacecraft split in two, and the *Eagle*, whose outer skin was a gold foil so delicate that a child could poke a hole into it, began

19

## The Far Side of the Moon

The far side of the moon is often referred to as the dark side. That really isn't an accurate description, because the sun shines on the moon, just as it does on Earth. However, the far side is permanently hidden from Earth and was not ever seen—even in a photograph—until 1959 when the Soviet space probe *Luna 3* flew by and took pictures. Those images revealed how different the two sides of the moon are from each other. The near side, which we see from Earth, is relatively smooth and is rich in minerals such as potassium and phosphorous, which are also found on Earth. The far side is much more mountainous and rough, and does not contain as many minerals. Scientists are eager to learn more about the far side of the moon through future missions.

its descent. There were only minutes' worth of fuel in the tank. A separate stage, or section, of the *Eagle* contained fuel to get back to the *Columbia*.

Back in Houston, Texas, at the Lyndon B. Johnson Space Center, anxious engineers used computers to guide the *Eagle* down to what they thought was a smooth area of the moon's surface. As the pilot, Neil Armstrong had the capability to override the computers if he thought he had to. As he scanned the moon's rapidly approaching surface, he was surprised. The area immediately below him wasn't smooth at all! It was littered with rocks and boulders. As quickly as he could, Armstrong pitched the small spacecraft forward until it cleared the approaching rocks. He was searching for a clear spot to land.

"Sixty seconds," said a voice from Mission Control. That meant Neil Armstrong had sixty seconds to land the *Eagle* before its fuel would run out. His heart was racing. Monitors on his body indicated his heart was beating a whopping 156 times a minute, compared with a normal heartbeat for an adult, which is between 60 and 90 beats a minute. Neil Armstrong was tense.

"Thirty seconds," said Mission Control.

After another agonizing second or two, Armstrong's voice came over the radio. "I found a good spot."

A relieved ground crew in Houston responded, "We copy you down, *Eagle.*"

Neil Armstrong settled the *Eagle* onto smooth basalt in the Sea of Tranquility. And then he spoke the words that were heard

# Why Do We See Only One Side of the Moon?

The moon rotates on its axis like a top, just as Earth does. However, the moon rotates more slowly than Earth, so a lunar "day" is much longer than a day on Earth. Earth rotates on its axis once every 24 hours. The moon rotates once every 27.3 days. It also completes an orbit of Earth in 27.3 days, so the two movements—the rotation of the moon on its axis and the moon's orbit of Earth—are synchronized. In other words, these two movements occur at the same rate of speed. One hemisphere of the moon (the near side) always faces Earth, while the other hemisphere (the dark side) always faces away.

The photographs at right, taken with cameras on board the Lunar Reconnaissance Orbiter (LRO), reveal the differences in the surfaces of the near and far sides of the moon. The upper left image shows the familiar near side of the moon, which is relatively smooth. In the upper right image, the moon has rotated on its axis 60 degrees. Middle left, the moon has rotated 120 degrees and the deeply cratered surface of the far side comes into view. The middle right image shows the far side of the moon, 180 degrees from the upper left image. On the lower left, the rotation is 240 degrees. The lower right is 300 degrees, and you can begin to see the familiar near side of the moon come into view.

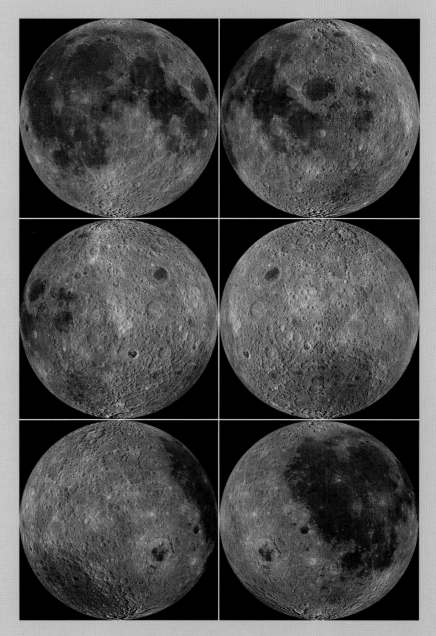

(NASA/Goddard/Arizona State University)

With less than thirty seconds to spare before the *Eagle*'s fuel would run out, Neil Armstrong found a smooth enough place to land on the moon. This is the first picture ever taken from the surface. (NASA)

As the *Eagle* sits safely on the Sea of Tranquility, Buzz Aldrin removes equipment for experiments from the landing craft's storage area. (NASA)

around the world: "Houston, Tranquility base here. The *Eagle* has landed."

The two men spent a few more hours on board the *Eagle* while Mission Control ran tests to make certain the spacecraft and its passengers weren't going to sink into the moon's surface, or the *Eagle* wasn't going to spring a leak. Then they were finally given permission to leave the relative safety of the craft. Neil Armstrong carefully climbed out of the *Eagle,* stood on the surface of the moon, and once again spoke historic words: "That's one small step for man, one giant leap for mankind."

As soon as he had taken his "one small step," Armstrong received his first order from Mission Control since leaving the *Eagle.* Before doing anything else, he was to stoop down and gather some rocks and soil and put them in his pocket. NASA was worried. No one had ever set foot on the moon before, and no one knew what to expect. If the astronauts had to leave in a hurry for any reason, the scientists wanted to be certain at least a few samples of lunar soil and rocks would make the return trip to Earth with them.

After 21 hours and 36 minutes, it was time for Neil Armstrong and Buzz Aldrin to leave the moon's surface and return home. But first they rested, sleeping for seven hours inside the *Eagle.* Then they fired the lunar module's engines, ascended from the lunar surface, and rejoined Mike Collins on board *Columbia.* By the time the two spacecraft joined up, or docked, Mike Collins was on his 27th orbit of the moon! On July 24,

When the crew of Apollo 11 left Earth, headed for the moon, they were dressed appropriately. Each of them wore a custom-made space suit, constructed of layers of Teflon-treated nylon and other kinds of cloth, and weighing 180 pounds! Of course, that was here on Earth. Once the crew broke free of Earth's gravity, the suit weighed nearly nothing.

Underneath their suits, the astronauts wore a liquid cooling and ventilation garment. Tubes allowed water and air to circulate, keeping the astronauts cool during the moon's day, when temperatures can soar as high as 250 degrees F, and warm at night, when temperatures could sink as low as –250 degrees F. When they were on the moon's surface, the astronauts wore a backpack that contained supplies of oxygen and water. A "Snoopy cap" with radio communication devices fit snugly over their heads, and then the helmet, which was a clear bubble, was screwed onto a neck ring at the top of the space suit. Special thermal gloves with silicone-rubber fingertips and protective boots completed their ensemble. Inside the spacecraft, the outer gloves, bubble helmet, and life-support system weren't needed and weren't worn.

1969, after a mission that had lasted 195 hours, 18 minutes, and 35 seconds, the crew of Apollo 11 splashed down into the Pacific Ocean, where a crew aboard the USS *Hornet* was waiting to recover them. The men and the moon rocks had made it home.

As it turned out, there was no need for NASA to worry about collecting samples. Eventually the combined flights of the Apollo program returned more than eight hundred pounds of moon rock and soil to Earth. Today planetary scientists pore over these samples as eagerly as they did almost fifty years ago. What they have learned has revealed much about the earliest days of the solar system, when Earth and the moon were forming.

A solar system is a group of planets, asteroids, comets, and other space objects that are in orbit around a star. These objects are formed from the debris that is left over after the star comes

Buzz Aldrin's boot left a print in the soft regolith of the moon's surface. (NASA)

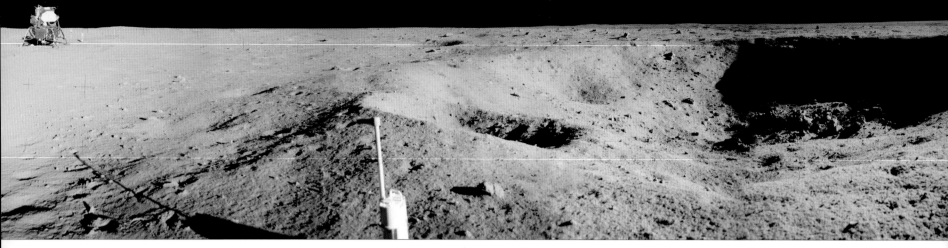

A small crater near the *Eagle* provided a rocky floor to explore. (NASA)

# The Landscape of the Moon

The near side of the moon has two basic landscapes—lowlands and highlands. You can see both from Earth with the naked eye. The lowlands are the dark areas, lunar basins called *maria*. The basins were formed by impacts early in the moon's history. Later, basalt, a dark volcanic rock, seeped into the basins and hardened. The light-colored areas of the moon are the *terrae*, or highlands. The highlands are the oldest surfaces on the moon, having formed soon after the moon came together. Unlike the smoother lowlands, the moon's highlands are peppered with craters left over from the early days of the moon's formation. The moon's "soil" is actually ground-up gray-black rock called regolith. It covers the entire surface of the moon, but unlike the soil on Earth, regolith has no organic, or living, materials in it to nourish plant life.

together and begins to "shine." A star shines after it has fused enough hydrogen into helium to release energy in the form of heat and light. Once our sun began to shine, about 4.5 billion years ago, the leftover material from its formation continued to whirl around it, and eventually spun itself into a flat, pancake-like shape called a protoplanetary disk. That whirling protoplanetary disk around our sun contained all the building blocks for everything in our solar system, including Earth and its moon.

The process of creating a solar system is not a gentle one. For about a half-million years after the sun began to shine, our new solar system was a pretty violent place. As the protoplanetary disk whirled, the meteoroids, asteroids, and other space debris within it were whizzing around too, pulled by the gravity of the sun. At times objects collided with one another like runaway bumper cars in a giant carnival ride, and in some cases the force of the collisions fused the smaller objects into the larger ones.

Sometimes, accretion fused enough material together to

form a planet. But in other collisions the larger objects simply destroyed the smaller ones, smashing their material back into grains of space dust. Earth was a still-forming 50-million-year-old planet during this period of intense bombardment, and it did not yet have a moon.

Then, when the young Earth was about 60 million years old—practically an infant in the timeline of our solar system's formation—it took a mighty hit. An object about the size of Mars, half the size of Earth, slammed into our planet. Astrophysicists call this object the impactor, and this theory of how the moon formed is called the giant impact theory. The impactor's collision with Earth was staggering—about 100 million times more powerful than the asteroid impact that helped to destroy Earth's

This artist's rendering of our solar system shows the eight planets; the Kuiper Belt, an icy region at the outer limits of our solar system that contains trillions of asteroids and comets and at least three dwarf planets—Pluto, Ceres, and Eris; and a comet, all in orbit around the sun. In reality, the planets are too far away from each other to be shown in any detail, so this image is not to scale. (NASA/JPL)

# Missions to the Moon

In 1959 the government of the Soviet Union sent the first unmanned mission to the moon. Its spaceship, *Luna 2*, made impact with the moon near Autolycus, a crater Riccioli named after a Greek mathematician who studied spheres. Since then, there have been dozens of successful missions to the moon by many countries, including China, Japan, and India. These missions have included orbiters and landers. The United States is the only country to have put a human on the moon. Six Apollo missions sent twelve astronauts to the moon between 1969 and 1972.

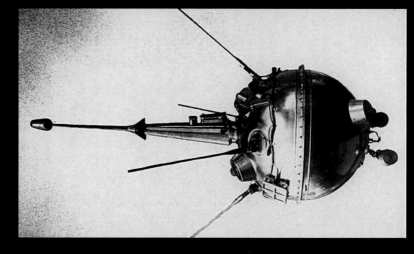

*Luna 2,* the first spacecraft to reach the moon. (NASA)

# Accretion

Our solar system is made up of eight planets and their moons—along with dwarf planets such as Pluto, Ceres, and Eris, and plenty of asteroids, comets, and other bits of space debris. All of these bodies began fracturing from collisions during the formation of our solar system. However, the planets and their moons are spheres, which means they are more or less round. They get their round shape by accretion. In accretion, every part of the object's surface is pulled evenly toward its center by the force of gravity. It is estimated that each of the planets in our solar system accreted rather quickly by astronomical standards—in about 10 to 35 million years! Asteroids and other, smaller space objects do not have enough gravity to pull them into a spherical, or round, shape, so their dimensions can be quite irregular, like the rocks on Earth.

An artist's rendering of the violent beginnings of our solar system. Note the protoplanetary disk whirling around the sun. (NASA/JPL-Caltech)

An artist's conception
of a planetary collision
similar to the one that
may have formed our moon.
(NASA/JPL)

dinosaur population millions of years later. According to the giant impact theory, the collision blew off a chunk of the young Earth and completely destroyed the impactor itself. Some of its material was absorbed into Earth, and the rest was turned into space debris. This collision turned some of the young Earth's outer layers into debris too, but since Earth was bigger and had more mass than the object that hit it, the rest of our planet survived, while the impactor did not.

Eventually the debris from the impactor and the debris from Earth's outer layers formed a ring of material that began to orbit Earth. And, similarly to the way planets themselves form from the material in a protoplanetary disk, the material in this ring around Earth began to accrete, forming the sphere that became our moon.

There have been other scientific theories about the formation of the moon, but today the giant impact theory is the one that is most widely accepted in the scientific community, and is supported by the information gained from studying the moon rocks. Earth and its moon have many of the same building blocks.

Of course, like all theories, this one could change. As future generations of scientists continue to study the moon rocks, their discoveries may lead to a different theory. But for now, there appears to be enough similarity between Earth and its moon to consider them members of the same family.

## Other Theories of the Moon's Formation

Before the Apollo missions, there were three major theories about the moon's formation. One proposed that Earth, which is larger than the moon and therefore has a stronger gravitational pull, "captured" the already formed moon and pulled it into its orbit. A second theory stated that Earth actually ejected, or threw off, the moon from itself. A third theory held that Earth and the moon formed separately, but very close to each other's position in space.

Some experts have also suggested that there were once two moons orbiting Earth but that they smashed into each other about 4.4 billion years ago and the smaller moon was absorbed into the moon we now have. In science today, new ideas are always welcome and old ideas can always be questioned. For now, the giant impact theory is considered accurate.

# CHAPTER THREE

# EARTH'S ATTIC

AN ATTIC IS A WONDERFUL place to explore. This space at the top of many houses is often used to store things that people no longer use. If the house is very old, the attic might be full of books, clothes, portraits, tools, and other items that tell a story of what the world was like when the house was newer.

In a way, the moon is like an attic. Closer to Earth than any other object in the solar system, the moon has remained nearly undisturbed since it formed. And like any good attic, our moon has stored clues, but to a much earlier time, billions of years ago, when the solar system was new. These clues from the moon can give geologists—scientists who study the composition of Earth—information about the earliest days of our planet too. That statement may seem strange. After all, if someone is interested in studying Earth's formation, why look to the moon? Why not study the ground right here under our feet? It seems like a logical question, but the truth is that in a way, Earth has

Our moon is Earth's closest companion in the solar system. (NASA)

31

Erosion has created amazing features in the Petrified Forest National Wilderness Area in Arizona. (National Park Service)

A Hawaiian volcano, now extinct. Centuries of erosion have worn away its exterior and exposed the interior walls. (Dr. Dwayne Meadows/NOAA)

disappeared. Nothing on Earth today is as it was when our planet formed more than four billion years ago, because Earth is dynamic, which means it is constantly changing.

Earth has heated up and cooled down several times over the ages. Land formed in one mass, then eventually broke apart into separate continents. Seas that covered parts of Earth dried up, exposing the soil below. Volcanoes began erupting from ocean floors, their lava forming islands where none existed before. Erosion and the slow creep of glaciers move surface soils away from their original locations. In addition, countless floods, tornadoes, droughts, wildfires, and earthquakes over time continue to change Earth's surface. Scientists estimate that approximately 80 percent of the current surface of our planet is less than 200 million years old, so Earth doesn't look at all like it did when our planet first formed. But the same is not true of our moon. Early in its formation, plenty of meteors hit the moon, forming its craters and altering its surface features, but that bombardment stopped after about a half-billion years—relatively quickly, in astronomical timelines. Like the attic of an undisturbed house, our moon has remained remarkably quiet for a long time—indeed, for the past 4 billion years or so—which makes it a perfect place to explore and seek clues to the conditions that existed in the early solar system.

Craters form when incoming pieces of space debris hit a planet or a moon's surface. In its beginning, the moon was hot—so hot, its surface was almost liquid, a soft crust of magma, or melted rock. As the early bombardment in the solar system continued, tens of thousands of pieces of space debris hit the moon. Although the incoming missiles may have been as irregular in shape as any rock, when they hit the crust, the shock waves, or energy, from the bomblike impact caused the crust to explode in a circular pattern.

All the terrestrial, or rocky, planets in our solar system have craters, because all of them were hit with space debris during the formation of the solar system. Although this period ended around 3.9 billion years ago, planetary scientists estimate that Earth and the other planets have continued to be hit, on average, by asteroids up to five miles long every million years or so, and a good hit leaves behind a crater as evidence.

Scientists estimate that fifty thousand years ago a meteorite

Crater 308, or Crater Daedalus, photographed by the crew of Apollo 11 as they flew past the far side of the moon. (NASA)

# Identified Flying Objects

There are lots of objects whizzing around in outer space—and they aren't the stars and planets. Meteors, meteoroids, meteorites, asteroids, and comets are part of this material.

**meteor:** What we think of as "shooting stars," a meteor is the flash we see in the night sky when a small chunk of space debris passes through Earth's atmosphere. "Meteor" describes the light, not the actual object.

**meteoroid:** The object, or debris, is called a meteoroid. Meteoroids, which are usually quite small, burn up as they enter Earth's atmosphere, creating the light we call a meteor.

**meteorite:** When a part of a meteoroid survives the trip through Earth's atmosphere and actually lands on our planet, it becomes a meteorite. Most meteorites are very small, but some can be as large as the one that created Meteor Crater.

**asteroids:** Generally larger than meteoroids, asteroids are pieces of rock that come from the asteroid belt, a region of space located between Mars and Jupiter.

**comets:** Comets are similar to asteroids except that they develop a fuzzy shell, because they are covered with ice and other compounds. They show an obvious tail when they orbit close to the sun.

# Parts of a Crater

Craters are holes that form on the surface of a moon or planet when it is hit with tremendous force by another object in space, called an impactor. When the impactor hits the surface, the heat and shock waves from the collision are enough to melt and vaporize the impactor, along with the surface debris—the impact ejecta—that is thrown up from the blow. A layer of the ejecta—the impact melt—forms the crater floor and the ring around the crater, creating a composite rock called breccia. Breccias form beneath the surface, too, caused by fracturing bedrock.

    Impact craters are divided into two types: simple and complex. Simple craters are usually deeper but smaller across than complex craters. They are shaped like small, rather smooth bowls. Like all bowl-shaped objects, craters have rims and walls. However, the walls of larger complex craters have collapsed downward and inward because of the effects of gravity—even the lesser gravity on the moon. In a complex crater, the force of the walls' collapse causes a central peak to form in the floor of the crater.

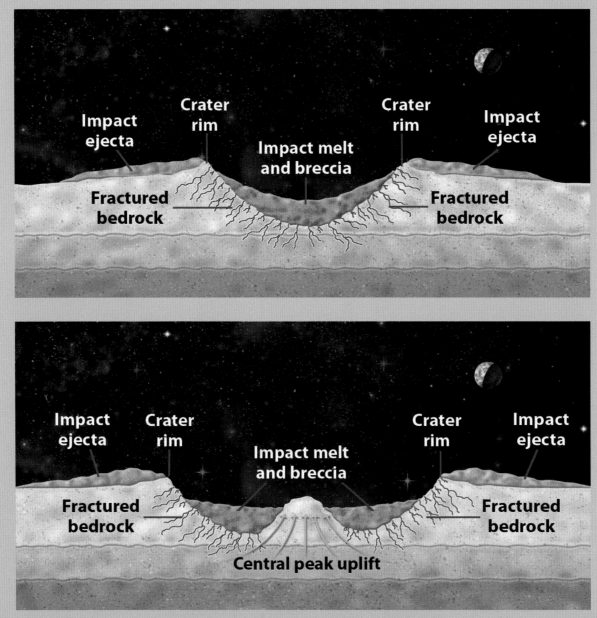

Simple crater (top) and complex crater. (Rob Schuster)

Meteor Crater (also known as Barringer Meteorite Crater) near Winslow, Arizona, is 570 feet deep and 4,100 feet across. It was created by an impact from a 130-foot-wide meteorite more than 50,000 years ago. (Jon Sullivan)

made of a combination of nickel and iron, traveling at about 26,000 miles per hour, smashed into the desert just north of the present city of Winslow, Arizona. Best estimates of the impact say it was as powerful as an explosion of more than 150 atom bombs! Meteor Crater is the enormous hole in Earth's crust that was left behind. Scientists and tourists from around the world visit it today. Although huge hits like the one that created Meteor Crater are once-in-a-million-year events, smaller meteorites can—and do—still hit Earth today. On February 15, 2013, a meteorite NASA estimated was the size of a bus and weighed about seven

# Retaining an Atmosphere

Gravity is the force that holds an atmosphere close to a planet. The more mass a planet has, the more gravity it has. Earth has enough mass and gravity to maintain a nice blanket of atmosphere that clings to our planet like sand sticks to bare wet feet. Mars, on the other hand, has half the mass of Earth, and therefore it has half the gravity of Earth; as a result, its atmosphere is quite thin. Until 2013, lunar scientists believed the moon was a perfect vacuum, meaning it had no atmosphere at all. They still consider it to be a near-perfect vacuum, but as they study the information that is constantly being returned to Earth from satellites orbiting the moon, they have reached a new conclusion: Our moon does have air; it's just extremely thin.

thousand tons exploded in the sky above Chelyabinsk, Russia. Most of its energy was absorbed into the atmosphere, but on the ground, thousands of people were hurt by exploding windows and flying debris as bits of the meteorite fell around the area.

Geologists love to study craters anywhere they can find them, because the giant holes expose layers of buried rock, and rocks always tell the story of how and when a planet or a moon formed.

While some have referred to the moon as Earth's attic, others have called it Earth's sister, because the currently accepted theory states that it formed from material spewed from Earth's crust when our planet was hit by the impactor. While it's true that Earth and the moon have many materials in common, as with siblings in any family, there are differences, too. A lot of the differences between Earth and its moon are due to atmosphere.

An atmosphere is the layers of gases that surround a planet and, in the case of Earth, protect it from the harmful rays of the sun, allowing life to flourish. Since the moon has practically no atmosphere, things are very different there.

Scientists occasionally refer to Earth as the Goldilocks planet. Just as Goldilocks finds her just-right chair, bowl of porridge, and bed in the three bears' cottage, Earth is a just-right distance from the sun—not too far, but not so close that its atmosphere burns up.

In addition to protecting our planet from the sun, Earth's atmosphere affects the colors we see. All color is contained in the sun's white light, or sunlight. Each color has a different wavelength. The reds have longer wavelengths than the blues. Objects on Earth absorb some of the wavelengths and reflect others. For example, an orange absorbs all the colors of the spectrum except orange. It reflects the orange wavelength. Our eyes pick up that reflected wavelength, send a signal to our brain, and just like that, we see an orange-colored fruit! Blue has a much shorter wavelength. When blue wavelengths hit the gas molecules in Earth's atmosphere, they get scattered in all directions—more than any other color—which is why we see a blue sky most of the time. Without an atmosphere thick enough to reflect and scatter sunlight, our sky would be black, just like the moon's.

Atmosphere affects sound, too. Like light, sound travels in waves, and when those sound waves reach our ears, we hear something, because the sound waves have vibrated the molecules in Earth's atmosphere. However, if there's no atmosphere to carry a sound wave, there won't be any sound to hear. Since the moon has almost no atmosphere, it's a quiet place indeed. When the Apollo 11 astronauts hammered the pole bearing the American flag into the moon's surface, the hammering was silent. When they walked across the moon's surface, their steps were silent too. You may wonder how the astronauts communicated with each other and Mission Control under those circumstances. Well, atmosphere is air, and there was just enough air inside their space helmets to allow sound waves to form. So they were able to use the radios built into their helmets to communicate with each other and with Mission Control back on Earth.

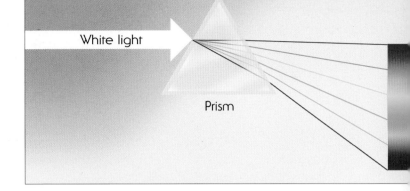

Sunlight, or white light, contains all the colors of the spectrum we can see—along with many we can't, such as ultraviolet light and radio waves. Three things are necessary in order to see color: light, an object, and vision. We see color because Earth's atmosphere acts like a prism, breaking sunlight into the visible colors of the spectrum, which are either absorbed by an object or reflected off of it. We "see" reflected, or refracted, light as a color. (Rob Schuster)

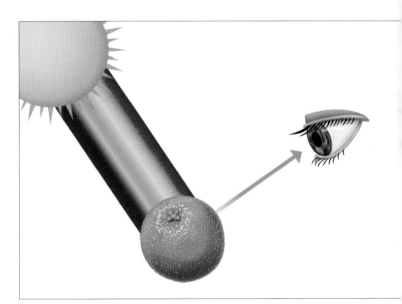

An orange looks orange because the fruit has absorbed all the wavelengths of light that are hitting it except for orange. That particular wavelength in the spectrum bounces back toward the eye, which then "sees" orange. If you were looking at the same fruit in a room with no light, it would not be orange. (Rob Schuster)

Earth's atmosphere shows as a
blue ribbon that surrounds the planet.
The moon is in the distance. (NASA/JPL)

Atmosphere affects how we see things too. Everything you see on Earth appears just a bit fuzzier here than it would on the moon. That's because not only does Earth's atmosphere surround our planet with a thin, transparent blanket of gas, it surrounds everything *on* Earth—rocks, trees, people, dogs, cats, and so forth. It isn't obvious, of course, because we have never known anything different, but no one sees anything on this planet with perfect clarity, because of the slight distortion caused by the atmosphere. However, if you were on the moon, everything you saw—the features on the rocks, the soil, the craters, the mountains and volcanoes—would be amazingly distinct and clear because the moon has such a thin atmosphere.

Even the horizons look different on Earth and our moon. On Earth, the horizon—the point where the sky meets the earth—appears as a flat line far in front of you. That is not so on the moon. If you look toward the lunar horizon, it curves, as if the ground is falling away from you. And the lack of atmosphere makes that horizon appear much closer than it actually is. Buzz Aldrin noticed this strange feature during his time on the moon and remarked, "Distances here are deceiving."

And finally, without a thick atmosphere, there can be no weather, so the moon has no rain, floods, winds, or erosion. The moon's extremely thin atmosphere is the reason its surface has remained almost unchanged for billions of years, silent and still, like an untouched attic just waiting to have its treasures discovered.

The Genesis Rock was found sitting on top of a pedestal of moon dirt, or regolith, as if waiting to be discovered. (NASA)

# CHAPTER FOUR

# THE MOON ROCKS

THE APOLLO MISSIONS were a result of a race between the United States and the former Soviet Union to see who could be first to put a person on the moon. Although Neil Armstrong and Buzz Aldrin had been ordered to pick up some samples from the lunar surface, serious collection of moon rocks was almost an afterthought—putting a man on the moon and returning him safely to Earth was the goal. However, once the United States had achieved this goal, scientists such as Dr. Robert M. Walker (1929–2004), who went on to found the Mc-Donnell Center for the Space Sciences at Washington University in St. Louis, Missouri, convinced NASA to build a laboratory to preserve the precious moon rocks and make them available for scientists from around the world to study. As a result, the astronauts of all the remaining Apollo missions went to work using tongs, scoops, rakes, hammers, and drills to collect samples from the moon and bring them back to Earth. As he recalled the day in 1969 when he and his team of physicists at the university

The first moon rocks, secured in sterile containers, arrive at the Lunar Receiving Laboratory in August 1969. (NASA)

first handled some of the moon rocks, Dr. Walker said, "We felt just like a bunch of kids who were suddenly given a brand-new toy store. . . . There was so much to do, we hardly knew where to begin."

It seems hard to imagine now, but before the moon rocks were brought to Earth, geologists were not at all certain what the surface of the moon was like. They weren't exactly sure how the moon formed, or even how old it was. The moon rocks answered those questions, because every rock—no matter where it is found—has a story to tell. And once the moon rocks were safely on Earth, they began to tell theirs.

Scientists determined the age of the moon by using a process called radioactive dating on the moon's rocks. Say, for instance, you wanted to calculate how long a glass of milk had been sitting on the kitchen counter. The time it takes milk to turn from fresh to sour and then to curdle, is its rate of decay. If you know how fast the atoms in milk break down, or decay, you could determine how long the milk had been sitting out on the counter—a half hour or several days. Though far more complex, radioactive dating works on the same principle.

Our sun beams out radiation in the form of heat and light throughout the solar system. Since its formation, the moon has been absorbing radiation from the sun, radiation that has been absorbed into its rocks and regolith. Scientists can tell how old a moon rock is by measuring how quickly the radioactivity in the rock has decayed. They can do this because they know how quickly specific atoms, called isotopes, decay. Some isotopes decay faster than others, but as long as scientists know the rate of decay for the isotope they are measuring, they can calculate how old an object is. Radioactive dating is extremely accurate and can be used to date organic material, such as mummies or fossils, and inorganic material, such as rocks.

Every Apollo mission landed on a different spot on the moon, and moon rocks were collected each time, so there is some variety in what was collected. The honor of finding the oldest moon rock went to two astronauts from the Apollo 15 mission—James Irwin and David Scott. Even though the men could not have fully realized the significance of their discovery at the time, it is obvious from the official NASA transcript of their conversation with Dr. Joseph P. Allen, who was at Mission Control in Houston, that they knew they had come upon something important. Their training as "amateur" geologists was paying off. The men

## Astronauts as Geologists

Geology is the study of the physical structure of Earth. Planetary geology—sometimes known as astrogeology—is the study of celestial bodies. Understanding how rocks form—whether they are on the moon, Earth, or anywhere else—is part of the study of geology. However, the first astronauts were not trained geologists; they were test pilots. If they were going to select moon rocks to return to Earth, they needed to understand something about geology and learn more about what they might see on the moon's surface. Because it was thought that parts of California, Hawaii, and New Mexico might resemble the landscape on the moon, astronauts went to those locations to study the rocks and train for their missions to the moon. An astronaut who was also an official geologist didn't go to the moon until the last manned mission, Apollo 17. He was astronaut-geologist Dr. Harrison "Jack" Schmitt.

Before their historic find on the moon, Apollo 15 astronauts Jim Irwin and Dave Scott trained for their mission by looking for rocks in New Mexico. Note, behind them, the mockup of the "moon buggy," a vehicle designed to transport them over the lunar landscape. The command module pilot, Alfred Worden, is not pictured. (NASA)

# NASA Transcript of the Moment
# the Genesis Rock Was Found

145:42:47 Scott: Guess what we just found. (Jim laughs with pleasure) Guess what we just found! I think we found what we came for.

145:42:53 Irwin: Crystalline rock, huh?

145:42:55 Scott: Yes, sir. You better believe it.

145:42:57 Allen: Yes, sir.

145:42:58 Scott: Look at the plage in there.

145:42:59 Irwin: Yeah.

145:43:00 Scott: Almost all plage.

145:43:01 Irwin: (Garbled)

145:43:02 Scott: As a matter of fact (Laughing) Oh, boy! I think we might have ourselves something close to anorthosite, 'cause it's crystalline, and there's just a bunch . . . It's just almost all plage. What a beaut.

145:43:18 Irwin: That is really a beauty. And, there's another one down there!

145:43:22 Scott: Yeah. We'll get some of these.

145:43:24 Allen: Bag it up!

145:43:27 Scott: Ah! Ah!

145:43:29 Irwin: Beautiful.

145:43:30 Scott: Hey, let me get some of that clod there. No, let's don't mix them. Let's make this a special . . . Why [don't] . . . I'll zip it up.

145:43:36 Irwin: Okay.

145:43:37 Scott: Make this bag, 196, a special bag.

145:43:40 Allen: Yes, sir.

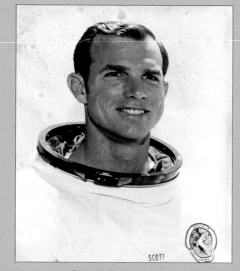

David Scott (NASA)

James Irwin (NASA)

All rocks, whether they are found on Earth or the moon, are made from various minerals. In this exchange with Mission Control, Dave Scott refers to finding a rock made from anorthosite and says it's full of "plage." An anorthosite rock is common on Earth and is full of a mineral called plagioclase feldspar, or plage for short. Finding anorthosite rocks on the moon helped scientists confirm their theory that our moon formed from material that was once part of Earth.

Jim Irwin working on the moon during the Apollo 15 mission. (NASA)

David Scott on the surface of the moon. (NASA)

On Earth, the Genesis Rock remains in carefully controlled conditions at the Lunar Sample Laboratory Facility at the Johnson Space Center. (NASA)

placed the moon rock in a bag they labeled 196. Bag 196 was special. As it turned out, Jim Irwin and Dave Scott had collected one of the oldest solid pieces of *anything* in our solar system. No rock on Earth—*nothing* on Earth—comes even close to being this old.

The rock that Dave Scott placed in bag 196 is now called the Genesis Rock. Geologists estimate that it formed 4.5 *billion* years ago. Here was a chance to learn more about the very beginning of our solar system! However, eager as they were to study the moon rocks, the scientists had to wait. The rocks, along with the Apollo 15 astronauts, had to go into quarantine as soon as they returned to Earth.

Quarantine is a period of isolation when a person or animal—or a rock, for that matter—is kept away from others in order to prevent the possible spread of disease. Since no one knew if there were strange bacteria in the moon rocks, NASA made elaborate preparations to store them in sterile conditions. The Lunar Receiving Laboratory, or LRL, was built at the Johnson Space Center, and at first the moon rocks were stored there. Later, when it was known that the moon rocks would not contaminate anyone who handled them, a new fear arose. The elements on Earth could contaminate the moon rocks and make them useless for study. So a new, even more secure building, the Lunar Sample Laboratory Facility, or LSLF, was also constructed at the Johnson Space Center and most, but not all, of the moon rocks are stored there today in stainless-steel cabinets.

Nitrogen gas blows over them at all times. The nitrogen has been processed to remove any trace of water or oxygen, because the moon rocks contain tiny amounts of elements that are found in rocks here on Earth, including microscopic amounts of iron. On Earth, when iron is exposed to water, rust forms. So if a moon rock contained a speck of iron and then was exposed to the molecules of water in Earth's atmosphere, rust would form, and that could affect the results of scientific experiments. If scientists want to learn anything from the moon rocks and soil, then those rocks and soil must be kept exactly as they were on the moon's surface.

Once it was determined that the moon rocks were not dangerous, it was time to study and share them with other scientific institutions around the world. The discoveries continue to this day. Not only have scientists been able to date the age of the moon by studying the decay of the radiation that is in the rocks; they have also used that radiation to understand more about our sun's activity in the earliest days of our solar system. Understanding how the sun behaved when it was a young star can provide clues to understanding how it may behave in the future as it grows older.

The radiation also revealed that the moon rocks vary in age. Although all were younger than the Genesis Rock, even the youngest of those collected probably formed 4 billion years ago. So, by dating the age of the Genesis Rock at 4.5 billion years, and the youngest moon rocks at about 4 billion years, scientists drew the conclusion that the early bombardments in our solar system

Scientists inspect the moon rocks at the Lunar Sample Laboratory Facility. (NASA)

Above and below: Artists' renditions of possible moon colonies. Note the lunar rover in the foreground above. (NASA)

probably stopped around 4 billion years ago. And by studying the fossil record here on Earth, they also know that was about the time life began to appear on our planet—not life as we know it, but in the form of single-cell organisms. Now scientists wonder, if life appeared on Earth soon after the solar system settled down, could it also have appeared on other, still undiscovered planets in our solar system? Studying the moon's rocks raises as many questions as it answers. The answer to the question of life arising on other planets in our solar system remains unknown. For now.

People dream of living on the moon, and if this is to happen, human beings will need practical ways to establish a colony there. The moon rocks and regolith are proving to be helpful in surprising ways. Lawrence A. Taylor is a professor of petrology and geochemistry at the University of Tennessee. Dr. Taylor was one of the scientists who advised the astronauts as they collected their samples from the moon, and he eagerly studied some of the lunar material that they brought back. He was especially interested in moon dust—the powdery grit that could get into anything humans wore while on the moon, including space suits or the visors on space helmets, or anything that humans put on the moon, such as machinery or habitats. Dr. Taylor decided to heat up some of the dusty regolith in a microwave oven, just to see what would happen. He put in a small amount and found that within thirty seconds the dust melted, or fused, itself into something solid. This process is called sintering, and it happened because the lunar dust contained microscopic beads of iron. Next, Dr. Taylor used his imagination and drew a sketch of something he called a "lunar lawnmower." In an interview with NASA, Dr. Taylor said, "Picture a buggy pulled behind a rover that is outfitted with a set of magnetrons. [A magnetron is the device that makes a microwave oven work.] With the right power and microwave frequency, an astronaut could drive along, sintering the soil as he goes, making a continuous brick half a meter deep—and then change the power settings to melt the top inch or two to make a glass road."

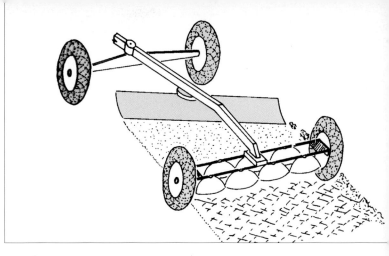

Dr. Lawrence Taylor's sketch of his "lunar lawnmower." (NASA)

There are other imaginative uses for the lunar soil. The moon's rocks and soil are rich in oxides, chemical compounds that combine atoms of oxygen with another element, like silicon or iron. When a material is heated to a certain point, it will break down into its atoms, so lunar dust that is rich in oxides can be heated to the point that the oxygen is released. The theory is that the oxygen could then be used by the early moon colonists for breathing, and to make rocket fuel, so their spaceships would have enough fuel to return them to Earth.

It takes imagination, coupled with education, to come up with ideas that would make it possible for human beings to live somewhere in our solar system beyond Earth's boundaries. Satellites are studying the moon now, returning new and exciting information that may allow human beings to not only return to the moon but establish an outpost there.

# RACING TO THE MOON

THERE IS NO DOUBT that the Apollo missions, which began in 1963 and ended in 1972, were some of the most exciting scientific explorations that human beings have ever accomplished. And like any worthy goal, they were achieved step by step, mission after mission.

The race to the moon, as it is often called, began on January 2, 1959, when Russia (then part of the USSR, or Union of Soviet Socialist Republics) sent its spacecraft, *Luna 1,* to fly by the moon. Not wanting to sit on the sidelines, a few months later, on March 3, 1959, the United States sent its own spacecraft, *Pioneer 4,* to execute a flyby of the moon. More missions by both countries followed, and eventually, with Apollo 11, the United States became the first and only country to put humans on the moon.

The astronaut crew of Apollo 17—Eugene Cernan, Ronald Evans, and Harrison Schmitt—became the last men to walk on the moon in that era, and when they returned to Earth on

Planting a flag can be a symbol of winning a race. The astronauts of Apollo 11 planted the U.S. flag on the moon, along with a plaque that reads HERE MEN FROM THE PLANET EARTH FIRST SET FOOT UPON THE MOON JULY 1969, A.D. WE CAME IN PEACE FOR ALL MANKIND. It was signed by the Apollo 11 astronauts Neil Armstrong, Buzz Aldrin, and Mike Collins, as well as the president of the United States at that time, Richard Nixon. The flag did not stand long; it was blown over by the exhaust from the *Eagle*'s takeoff. (LPI)

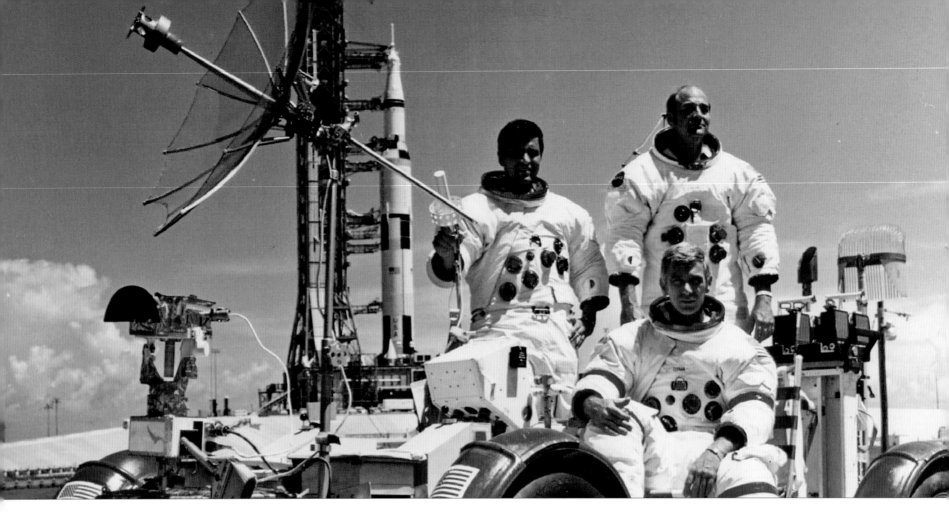

The last men to visit the moon (*left to right*: Harrison Schmitt, Ronald Evans, and Eugene Cernan) posed in their lunar rover before their 1972 mission. The Saturn rocket that launched them on their journey is seen in the background. (NASA)

December 19, 1972, that exciting period of exploration came to an end. But it was not the end of the dream of returning to the moon one day and establishing an outpost there. And the dream was contagious; other countries wanted to explore the moon too.

Japan sent its spacecraft, *Kaguya* (also known as *SELENE*), into lunar orbit in 2007 in order to map the moon in preparation for its own landings there. In 2008, India hoped to orbit the moon for two years with its spacecraft, *Chandrayaan-1,* but lost contact with it after it had spent only a week in orbit. China created its own space program, named Chang'e, after the young girl with her rabbit—the one Mike Collins referred to as the "bunny girl" as he spoke with Mission Control on the historic day men landed on the moon. China launched *Chang'e 2* in October 2010. This continuing mission is taking very accurate pictures of the moon's surface so the Chinese can select a suitable landing site for the lander and rover they plan to send to the moon in the near future.

Meanwhile, the United States has been hard at work too, with NASA creating more lunar missions using satellites and robots, rather than human beings, to return information. On June 18, 2009, two spacecraft were launched together aboard the *Atlas V* rocket: the Lunar Reconnaissance Orbiter, or LRO, and the Lunar Crater Observation and Sensing Satellite, or LCROSS. The job of the LRO was to orbit the moon, mapping its surface and looking for landing sites that might have a supply of resources such as minerals, and perhaps even water, that could be used by future colonists. Its companion spacecraft, LCROSS, was designed to look for evidence of water in the form of ice on the moon's surface.

LCROSS had two parts. One, called a shepherding spacecraft, was attached to another landing craft called the *Centaur*. The shepherding spacecraft guided the *Centaur* to an exact location, then released it to crash into the moon at that spot. As debris from the crash site rose up, the shepherding spacecraft flew through the debris, or ejecta, while its cameras and other

The *Atlas V* rocket headed to the moon, carrying LRO and LCROSS. (NASA/Tom Farrar, Kevin O'Connell)

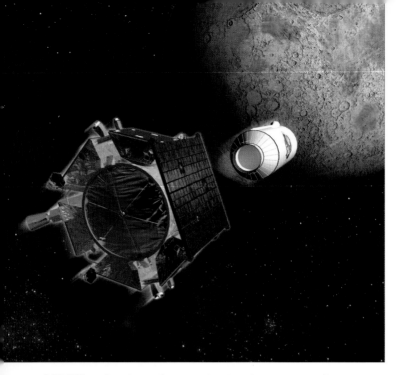

LCROSS at the time of separation into its two parts, the *Centaur* rocket and the shepherding spacecraft. Artist's rendering. (NASA)

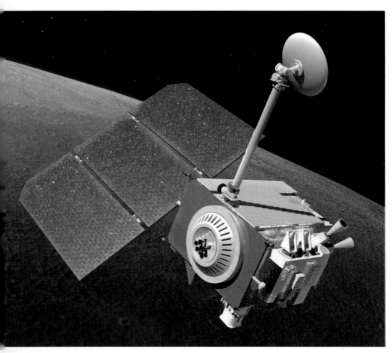

An artist's rendering of the LRO. (NASA's Goddard Space Flight Center)

instruments snapped pictures and gathered data. This information was relayed back to Mission Control before, just minutes later, the shepherding spacecraft also crashed into the moon's surface, creating a second debris plume and ending the existence of LCROSS. LRO continues to orbit the moon, recording and transmitting a wealth of information back to Earth.

So, what have we learned from the LRO and LCROSS? The analysis of the ejecta sent up by the crash of the *Centaur* stunned scientists around the world. Anthony Colaprete was a project scientist on the LCROSS mission, and he confirmed what scientists had suspected but had not been able to prove: the moon has water. Spectrometers and photometers on board the spacecraft detected and measured the grains of material in the plumes of debris. "We are ecstatic," he said. "Multiple lines of evidence show water was present."

It was 2009 when Colaprete spoke, and at that time no one had any idea exactly how much water was on the moon—just discovering it was exciting enough. However, in the summer of 2013, NASA was able to release an image of that water, based on maps made by the still-orbiting LRO. It seems the moon has much more water in its soil than anyone had thought. And it is not just contained within ice at the moon's poles, either, as everyone had previously assumed. Water is distributed across the moon's surface—not in oceans, rivers, and seas as it is on Earth, but in atoms of hydrogen and oxygen locked in the regolith. It spreads from the equator all the way to the poles!

Scientists have always said, "Where there's water, there's life," but the water on the moon doesn't seem to indicate life of any kind. Still, the discovery is encouraging. If there is water on the moon, it could be used to support life for astronauts living there. It could be used to irrigate greenhouse plants, and it could even be separated into its basic elements of hydrogen and oxygen. Human space explorers could use that oxygen to breathe, and the hydrogen could be used to make jet fuel to carry space travelers back to Earth. Water's presence on the moon makes the possibility of establishing a human outpost much less like science fiction than ever before.

On September 10, 2011, in a new mission, NASA launched twin spacecraft called "A" and "B" and sent them into a circular orbit 34 miles above the poles of the moon. The mission's name was GRAIL, which stands for Gravity Recovery and Interior Laboratory, and its purpose was to create an accurate map of the moon's surface and interior structure by measuring and mapping its gravitational field. A gravitational field is the space that surrounds any object that has mass—it's where the force of gravity is felt, and that force can be measured. The gravity, or attraction, between two objects is stronger when the objects are close together, and it weakens as the distance between them grows.

Planetary scientists knew that the moon had surface features, like mountains, basins, and craters. They all have a gravitational field, and if the gravitational field of each could be measured,

LCROSS scientists Anthony Colaprete and Dr. Kim Ennico study the results of the impact. (Dominic Hart/NASA Ames)

Anthony Colaprete from NASA confirms the presence of water on the moon. (NASA)

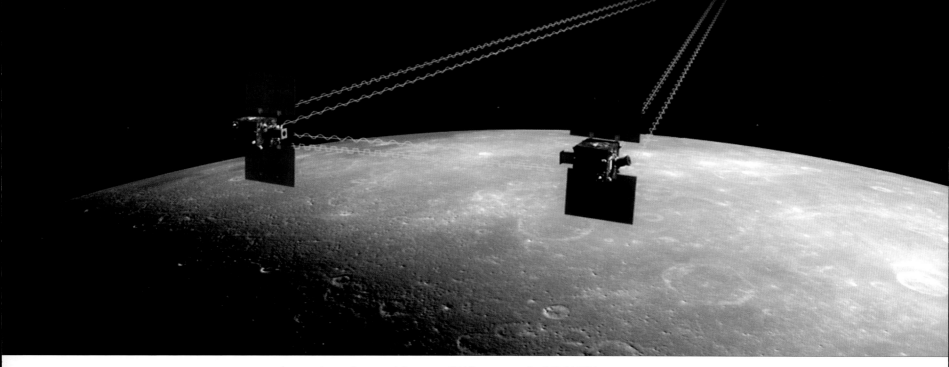

An artist's rendering of the twin GRAIL spacecraft. (NASA/JPL)

the height of the mountains and the depth of craters and basins would be revealed. To get the measurements, the two spacecraft continually orbited the moon's poles, while instruments on board sent out a radio signal, or beam, toward the moon's surface. As the spacecraft passed over the different surface features, the radio beams became shorter or longer, due to the different gravitational pulls from mountains, basins, and craters. Clefts hidden beneath the lunar surface also changed the radio beam's length. As each craft flew over these areas of greater and lesser gravity, it moved slightly toward and away from the other.

# Ebb and Flow and Sally Ride

Naming spacecrafts "A" and "B" isn't very exciting. The principal investigator for GRAIL, Professor Maria Zuber of the Massachusetts Institute of Technology, knew that. A contest began, and she said, "We asked the youth of America to assist us in getting better names." Fourth-grade students from the Emily Dickinson Elementary School in Bozeman, Montana, suggested Ebb and Flow, and they won the contest. Dr. Zuber said, "We chose Ebb and Flow because it's the daily example of how the moon's gravity is working on the Earth." The moon's gravity pulls on the surface of Earth's oceans, causing the inward and outward motions—the ebb and flow—of their tides.

Sally Ride was the first female astronaut from the United States to head into space. She was interested in the GRAIL program and suggested that special cameras be installed on A and B—before they were known as Ebb and Flow. The cameras were called MoonKAMS, which stood for Moon Knowledge Acquired by Middle School Students. Students from around the world were invited to submit requests to the GRAIL MoonKAM Missions Operation Center (MOC) asking that the cameras take pictures of areas of the lunar surface that they wanted to study. In all, there were more than 115,000 different photographs taken at the request of the students and posted on the GRAIL MoonKAM website for anyone who was interested to look at and study.

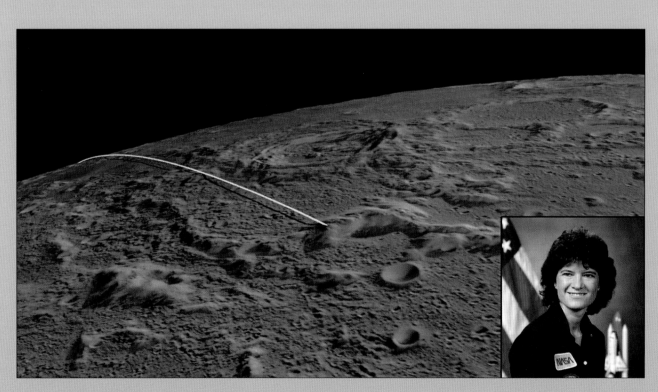

The Ebb and Flow crash site on the moon is named the Sally K. Ride Impact Site. (NASA/JPL-Caltech)

Earth's moon from space. The orange-colored band is Earth's troposphere, the lowest and most dense part of the atmosphere that protects the planet. (NASA)

The differences in the speed of each helped scientists create a very accurate map of the moon's gravitational field.

When this information was analyzed by NASA, the investigators came to some surprising conclusions. The crater on the moon that most of us have named "the Man on the Moon" (and which is officially called the Ocean of Storms, or *Oceanus Procellarum*) may not have been caused by a massive asteroid hit, as was previously thought. Instead, the measurements of its gravitational field seemed to suggest that the *mare* was the result of some internal force deep inside the early moon that generated heat and pushed melted rock through the moon's crust. If proved correct, that information would indicate the moon was far more active internally during its early development than many had thought. The information is still being studied, and it could change current theories about how the moon was formed.

Scientific research is exciting, because new knowledge is always uncovered in the process. Just a few years ago, all the books about the moon claimed it was a dry and airless place. No one dreamed there could be any kind of atmosphere or any kind of water there. But scientists must always be willing to let go of long-held beliefs if new information presents itself. Our moon is quite different from what we thought it was. It isn't dry and airless. It has water and atmosphere. Not like Earth's, but they're there. And those recent discoveries have led to more questions. How did the water get to the moon? Was it brought there by solar wind? Or by comets or asteroids? Or did it originate deep within the moon itself? These are questions waiting for answers.

The recent discovery of the moon's atmosphere, no matter how thin and fragile it is, raises questions too. The molecules in Earth's atmosphere are crowded together, giving us a nice, thick blanket of air. The molecules in the moon's atmosphere are so far apart, they rarely even touch each other, so the atmosphere is thin and fragile. The moon's atmosphere contains minerals such as sodium and potassium, which are not found in the air on Earth. Where did those minerals come from?

Though the molecules in the moon's atmosphere rarely touch

NASA's *Dawn* spacecraft took this close-up image of the giant asteroid Vesta. The asteroid could have an atmosphere similar to that on the moon. (NASA/JPL-Caltech/UCAL/MPS/DLR/IDA)

An early-morning meteor shower lights up the skies over Italy. (NASA/Antonio Finazzi)

each other, they do collide with the surface of the moon, so this kind of atmosphere is called a surface boundary exosphere, or SBE for short. Planetary scientists think SBEs may be the most common type of atmosphere in our solar system. They theorize that in addition to our moon, Mercury, some of the larger asteroids, many of the moons of other planets, and even some of the distant Kuiper Belt Objects, such as Pluto, may have SBEs too.

LADEE (the Lunar Atmosphere and Dust Environment Explorer) launched on September 6, 2013, and the mission ended on April 18, 2014. Its purpose was to learn more about the moon's strange atmosphere and the lunar dust. During their time on the moon, the Apollo astronauts talked about the lunar dust they encountered. It stuck to everything—their space suits, their instruments, everything! An instrument on board LADEE, called the LDEX, or Lunar Dust Experiment, discovered that some of the lunar dust was caused by the action of interplanetary micrometeoroid material—tiny, tiny rocklike particles—that were smashing into the surface of the moon as it sped through space, much like bugs hit a car window as it speeds down the road. With such a thin atmosphere on the moon, the particles went straight through, hit the lunar surface, and sent plumes of ejecta, or dust, back up into the thin "air." These types of particles head for Earth, too, but Earth has a thick atmosphere that burns up nearly all of them. However, sometimes we can spot them streaking through the night sky. When we see this, we call it a meteor shower.

LADEE also revealed that the lunar atmosphere, in addition to containing sodium and potassium, had evidence of three gases—helium, neon, and argon. And LADEE's experiments indicated that the helium and neon were supplied to the moon by the solar wind. That discovery raised even more questions.

The impacts that brought prebiotic material to the moon may also have brought the same type of cosmic material to Earth. Prebiotic is a term that means "before life." We do not think there has ever been life on the moon. But we definitely know there is life on Earth! So how did life here begin? Did it start with the arrival of the same kind of prebiotic material that is on the moon? If so, could that material have been carried somewhere else in the universe? And even if it was, did any type of life develop? These are huge questions that have no scientific answers for now. But that doesn't mean there won't be answers in the future.

As Earth's closest companion, the moon has much to teach us. In anticipation of his famous journey to the moon, Neil Armstrong said, "I think we're going to the moon because it's in the nature of the human being to face challenges. It's by the nature of his deep inner soul. We're required to do these things just as salmon swim upstream."

Darby Dyar, a professor of astronomy at Mount Holyoke

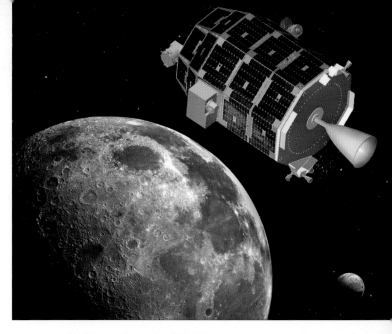

NASA art depicting LADEE as it approaches the moon's exosphere. (NASA)

Dr. Darby Dyar is conducting research to understand how hydrogen and oxygen—the two elements that create water—are distributed throughout the solar system. (NASA/Nola Taylor Redd)

One day humans will again stand on the surface of the moon and gaze back at Earth. (NASA/Goddard Space Flight Center)

College, reminds us that today, the thought of going to the moon to live is as strange as the thought of going to the New World must have been to the Europeans who lived 600 years ago. "They had been there a few times, but it took courage to send people there to stay," she says.

However, before anyone can stay on the moon, scientists will have to figure out how to get enough water to sustain life there. "We have to understand how water got to the moon, how much is still there, and how hard it would be to extract water for human consumption for a settlement," says Dr. Dyar. That research is going on right now. Dr. Dyar is part of a new NASA research program called the Solar System Exploration Research Virtual Institute. All across the country, researchers are trying to solve the problems that future colonists will face: getting water, growing food, creating adequate shelter, fueling the spaceships. Dr. Dyar believes that we can solve those problems, and that humans will return to the moon to stay within the next fifty years.

But which humans will be first to return to the moon? No one country owns Earth's satellite. It is there, waiting to be visited, by any country in the world that has the knowledge, the courage, and the will to figure out how to do it.

It will be difficult for us to return to the moon—almost as difficult as it was to get there in the first place. But as Neil Armstrong said, human beings are built to face challenges and surmount them. Our moon has more to tell us, and we humans will never stop exploring. It's the way we are made.

Our moon, in a
photo returned by
the *Galileo* spacecraft
in 1989. (NASA/JPL)

# GLOSSARY

**accretion:** The formation of a large solar-system object as gravity attracts nearby material, making the object larger while pulling all its material toward an inward central point, turning the object into a sphere, or ball.

**anorthosite:** A type of granular rock composed primarily of plagioclase feldspar.

**apogee:** The point in the orbit of a moon or other satellite at which it is farthest from Earth.

**astrophysicist:** An astronomer who studies the physical nature of stars and other celestial bodies.

**atmosphere:** The layer of gases that surrounds a planet, moon, or star.

**atom:** Submicroscopic building block of most substances or matter; the smallest particle of a substance that can exist.

**bacteria:** Tiny single-cell organisms; can be harmful or helpful.

**basin:** An indented formation where the sides slope toward the center.

**blue moon:** A second full moon in a calendar month.

**cell:** The basic unit of all living matter.

**Columbia:** The command and service module (CSM) that remained in orbit around the moon during the Apollo 11 mission; not to be confused with the later space shuttle of the same name.

**crater:** A bowl-shaped depression in a planet or a moon, usually caused by meteorites. A crater can also be formed by the action of a volcano.

**dark side of the moon:** The part of the moon that never faces Earth. Also known as the far side of the moon.

**debris:** Material left after an impact.

**drought:** A period of time when little or no rain falls.

**dynamic:** Constantly moving or changing.

**Eagle:** The lunar module that carried the Apollo 11 astronauts to the moon's surface.

**element:** A substance made of atoms of one kind; so basic that it cannot be changed into a simpler substance by ordinary methods. All matter is made up of elements.

**engraving:** A print made from a metal plate that has images or words etched into it.

**erosion:** The process of wearing away surface matter such as land or rocks, usually by wind, water, or ice.

**fallacy:** A failure in reasoning that makes an argument incorrect.

**finite:** Anything with definite limits that can be measured.

**Genesis Rock:** Oldest rock found on the moon, dating from the beginning of our solar system.

**geocentric:** Centered on Earth.

**geologist:** A scientist who studies what Earth is made of and how it was formed.

**glacier:** A large sheet of ice that slowly moves across the surface of the land.

**heliocentric:** Centered on the sun.

**highlands:** Mountainous areas of the moon. See also *terrae.*

**horizon:** The point in the distance where the sky appears to meet the land or sea.

**impactor:** A celestial object, such as a meteorite, asteroid, or comet, that collides with another celestial object.

**inorganic:** Matter, such as a rock, that is not a living thing or made from a living thing.

**iron:** A chemical element and metal that has great strength and will rust when exposed to water.

**isotope:** Atoms with the same number of protons but a different number of neutrons.

**Kuiper Belt Objects:** Any of the small icy bodies orbiting the sun in a distant region of swirling material called the Kuiper Belt. Most have a diameter smaller than Pluto, named a large Kuiper Belt Object or KBO.

**laboratory:** A place for scientific research and experimentation.

**lens:** A piece of glass (or plastic) that has been curved in order to either spread apart or bring together rays of light that pass through it.

**lowlands:** Floors of the basins on the side of the moon facing Earth. See also *maria*.

*Luna 2:* The first spaceship to land on the moon, launched by the Union of Soviet Socialist Republics (USSR).

**lunar:** Relating to the moon.

**magma:** Molten, or melted, rock.

**magnetron:** A device for converting electricity into short radio waves called microwaves. Magnetrons produce microwave radiation.

*maria* (singular, *mare*): Latin word meaning "seas" used to identify the dark, water-free floors of the craters, or basins, on the moon.

**megaton:** A unit of explosive power equal to one million tons of TNT.

**meteor:** An object from space that enters Earth's atmosphere, appearing as a streak of light.

**meteorite:** A meteor once it hits Earth's surface.

**meteoroid:** An object moving through space that would become a meteor if it entered Earth's atmosphere.

**mineral:** A solid, inorganic substance formed by nature that was never an animal or a plant.

**Mission Control:** The center of operations where space flights are guided and controlled.

**mission:** Objectives and plans for a space flight, manned or unmanned.

**molecule:** Two or more atoms bound together.

**moon:** A sphere orbiting another celestial body.

**moon rock:** Samples of rock taken from the lunar surface and brought to Earth.

**NASA:** National Aeronautics and Space Administration, a U.S. government agency charged with the peaceful exploration of space.

**near side of the moon:** The part of the moon always turned toward Earth.

**nitrogen:** A colorless, odorless gas that makes up more than three-quarters of Earth's atmosphere.

**northern hemisphere:** The half of a planet north of its equator.

**orbit:** The path a celestial object follows as it travels around another object.

**organic:** Living matter or material.

**oxide:** A combination of oxygen with some other chemical element.

**oxygen:** A colorless, odorless gas that makes up one-fifth of Earth's atmosphere.

**perigee:** The point in the orbit of a moon or other satellite at which it is closest to Earth.

**phases of the moon:** The shapes of the visible part of the moon, which change over the course of the moon's orbit around Earth.

**plagioclase feldspar:** A type of mineral found in certain rocks on Earth and the moon.

**planetary geology:** The geology of the celestial bodies such as the planets and their moons, asteroids, comets, and meteorites. Also known as astrogeology.

**protoplanetary disk:** Whirling disk of material that is left over after a star forms and may contain enough space debris to form a solar system.

**quarantine:** A period of isolation and separation, often to prevent the spread of disease.

**radioactive dating:** A process of determining the age of an object by measuring rate of decay, or the rate at which an isotope loses subatomic particles.

**refract:** To bend or change the direction of light, as when it passes through a lens or prism.

**regolith:** Ground-up lava, dirt, broken rock, and other loose, nonliving materials that cover solid rock on the surfaces of Earth or the moon.

**sinter:** To heat particles until they fuse together to make a solid mass.

**solar system:** A system of planets, moons, asteroids, comets, and other space debris in orbit around a star.

**southern hemisphere:** The half of a planet that is south of its equator.

**spectrometer:** An instrument that splits light collected from a telescope into the colors of the spectrum, allowing astronomers to detect the temperature, direction, speed, and weight of the object studied.

**sphere:** A round object, such as a ball or globe, whose curved edges are equally distant from its center.

**surface boundary exosphere:** An extremely thin layer of atmosphere that contains a few molecules of the lightest gases, such as hydrogen and perhaps some helium, lying close to a celestial object's surface.

**syllogism:** A form of reasoning in which a logical conclusion can be drawn from two statements.

**telescope:** A device that uses lenses and mirrors to make objects seem larger and closer than they are.

***terrae* (singular, *terra*):** A Latin word meaning "earth," used to identify the highlands of the moon.

**terrestrial:** Planets that have solid, rocky surfaces.

**theory:** An explanation based on reason and/or science that describes how or why something happens.

**tide:** The rise and fall of the level of an ocean, caused by the gravity from the sun and the moon.

**valley:** A low area of land that lies between hills or mountain ranges.

**volcano:** A vent or hole in the crust of a planet or moon from which lava and gases erupt or have erupted in the past.

**waning:** Phases of the moon during which it appears to be getting smaller.

**waxing:** Phases of the moon during which it appears to become larger.

The surface of the moon, photographed by the Lunar Orbiter 2 spacecraft in 1966. (NASA Lunar Orbiter Recovery Project)

# FURTHER READING

## BOOKS

Aldrin, Buzz. Illustrated by Wendell Minor. *Reaching for the Moon.* New York: HarperCollins, 2005.

Asimov, Isaac. *The Solar System: The Moon.* New York: Prometheus Books, 2003.

Floca, Brian. *Moonshot: The Flight of* Apollo 11. New York: Atheneum/Richard Jackson Books, 2009.

Lassieur, Allison. *The Moon Exposed.* Minnesota: Heinemann-Raintree, 2006.

Ross, Stewart. *Moon: Science, History, and Mystery.* New York: Scholastic, 2009.

Simon, Seymour. *The Moon.* New York: Simon and Schuster Books for Young Readers, 2003.

Thimmish, Catherine. *Team Moon: How 400,000 People Landed* Apollo 11 *on the Moon.* Boston: Houghton Mifflin Books for Children, 2006.

## WEBSITES

The First Men on the Moon: The *Apollo 11* Lunar Landing
www.firstmenonthemoon.com

*Experience the* Apollo 11 *lunar landing as experienced by the astronauts and flight controllers through video, audio, and other data.*

Google Moon
www.google.com/moon

*Tour the lunar landing sites, narrated by Apollo astronauts.*

The Moon: Zoom Astronomy—Enchanted Learning
www.enchantedlearning.com/subjects/astronomy/moon/

*Explore the moon and learn about its phases and its effect on Earth's tides.*

National Aeronautics and Space Administration
www.nasa.gov

*Explore the universe and learn from all of NASA's missions of discovery.*

Solar System Exploration: Planets: Earth's Moon
www.solarsystem.nasa.gov/planets/profile.cfm?Object=Moon

*Learn how our moon makes Earth a livable planet.*

Starchild: A Learning Center for Young Astronomers
starchild.gsfc.nasa.gov/docs/StarChild/StarChild.html

*Information and activities related to space, astronomy, and the solar system, organized by age groups.*

# INDEX

Note: Page numbers in **bold** type refer to photos or illustrations and their captions.